I0191821

ON PURPOSE

LEADER GUIDE

On Purpose:
Finding God's Voice in Your Passion

On Purpose
978-1-7910-2970-8
978-1-7910-2969-2 *eBook*

On Purpose: DVD
978-1-7910-2973-9

On Purpose: Leader Guide
978-1-7910-2971-5
978-1-7910-2972-2 *eBook*

Also by Magrey R. deVega
Questions Jesus Asked
The Bible Year
Almost Christmas (with Ingrid McIntyre,
April Casperson, & Matt Rawle)
Hope for Hard Times
Savior
Embracing the Uncertain
One Faithful Promise
Five Marks of a Methodist

Also by Jevon Caldwell-Gross
The Big Picture (with Nicole Caldwell-Gross)

Also by Susan Robb
Called
Seven Words
The Angels of Christmas
Remember (Coming December 2023)

Also by Sam McGlothlin
Advent: A Calendar of Devotions 2023

**MAGREY R. DEVEGA, SAM MCGLOTHLIN,
JEVON CALDWELL-GROSS, SUSAN ROBB**

ON PURPOSE

Finding **God's Voice**
in **Your Passion**

LEADER GUIDE

Abingdon Press | Nashville

On Purpose
Finding God's Voice in Your Passion
Leader Guide

Copyright © 2023 Abingdon Press
All rights reserved.

No part of this work may be reproduced or transmitted in any form or by any means, electronic or mechanical, including photocopying and recording, or by any information storage or retrieval system, except as may be expressly permitted by the 1976 Copyright Act, the 1998 Digital Millennium Copyright Act, or in writing from the publisher. Requests for permission can be addressed to Rights and Permissions, The United Methodist Publishing House, 810 12th Avenue South, Nashville, TN 37203-4704 or emailed to permissions@abingdonpress.com.

978-1-7910-2971-5

Scripture quotations unless noted otherwise are from the Common English Bible. Copyright © 2011 by the Common English Bible. All rights reserved. Used by permission. www.CommonEnglishBible.com.

MANUFACTURED IN THE
UNITED STATES OF AMERICA

CONTENTS

TO THE LEADER

We are hungry for a sense of purpose, direction, and calling in our lives. That's as basic an ingredient to the human experience as they come. We want to be part of something bigger than ourselves. We want to participate in something that has eternal merit and lasting impact. We do not want to live a shallow, hollow existence. We yearn for deeper meaning, for deeper purpose within our lives. We want to be more than we are.

On Purpose: Finding God's Voice in Your Passion is a four-part exploration of the spiritual principles that allow us to listen to God, discover our purpose and passion, join with others in the journey, and ultimately, make a difference in the world around us. As you study the book together with those in your small group, you will learn to minimize the barriers that prevent us from listening to God and recalibrate your spiritual lives to be more in tune with who God is and how God is calling you. You will discover that listening together, in the context of community, not only helps us be part of something bigger than ourselves: God will use us to have an impact in the world far greater than the sum of our parts.

How to Facilitate This Study

This four-session study makes use of the following components:

- the book, *On Purpose: Finding God's Voice in Your Passion*, by Magrey R. deVega, Sam McGlothlin, Jevon Caldwell-Gross, and Susan Robb;
- this Leader Guide; and
- *On Purpose: Finding God's Voice in Your Passion* DVD or a subscription to Amplify Media to access the streaming videos (www.amplifymedia.com).

You will need a DVD player or computer and a television or projection screen so that you can watch the DVD segments as part of your group session. If you or your church has a subscription to Amplify Media, use your login and find the videos by searching for *On Purpose*. Participants in the study will also need access to Bibles during the session. Finally, this study encourages the use of journals or notebooks to help participants reflect on their lives. *Ask each participant to bring a journal or notebook to your session each week and bring one or two extras in case someone forgets.*

Each session is structured into a 60-minute format and contains the following sections:

- Planning the Session (contains session objectives, biblical foundation passages, and preparation steps to take)
- Opening Activity and Prayer (5 minutes)
- Watch DVD Segment (10 minutes)
- Study and Discussion (35–40 minutes)
- Closing Activity and Prayer (5 minutes)

This study is designed to help individuals hear God's voice and discern God's call through their gifts, passions, and others around them. At several points in each session, participants will be invited to write responses in a journal or notebook.

Helpful Hints

Preparing for Each Session

- Pray for wisdom and discernment from the Holy Spirit, for you and for each member of the group, as you prepare for the study.
- Before each session, familiarize yourself with the content. Read the study book chapter again.
- Choose the session elements you will use during the group session, including the specific discussion questions you plan to cover. Be prepared, however, to adjust the session as group members interact and as questions arise. Prepare carefully but allow space for the Holy Spirit to move in and through the group members and through you as facilitator.
- Prepare the space where the group will meet so that the space will enhance the learning process. Ideally, group members should be seated around a table or in a circle so that all can see one another. Movable chairs are best so that the group can easily form pairs or small teams for discussion.

Shaping the Learning Environment

- Create a climate of openness, encouraging group members to participate as they feel comfortable.
- Remember that some people will jump right in with answers and comments, while others need time to process what is being discussed.
- If you notice that some group members seem never to be able to enter the conversation, ask them if they have thoughts to share. Give everyone a chance to talk but keep the conversation moving. Moderate to prevent a few individuals from doing all the talking.
- Communicate the importance of group discussions and group exercises.
- If no one answers at first during discussions, do not be afraid of silence. Count silently to ten, then say something such as, "Would anyone like to go first?" If no one responds, venture an answer yourself and ask for comments.
- Model openness as you share with the group. Group members will follow your example. If you limit your sharing to a surface level, others will follow suit.
- Encourage multiple answers or responses before moving on to the next question.
- Ask: "Why?" or "Why do you believe that?" or "Can you say more about that?" to help continue a discussion and give it greater depth.
- Affirm others' responses with comments such as, "Great" or "Thanks" or "Good insight"—especially

if it's the first time someone has spoken during the group session.

- Monitor your own contributions. If you are doing most of the talking, back off so that you do not train the group to listen rather than speak up.
- Remember that you do not have to have all the answers. Your job is to keep the discussion going and encourage participation.

Managing the Session

- Honor the time schedule. If a session is running longer than expected, get consensus from the group before continuing beyond the agreed-upon ending time.
- Involve group members in various aspects of the group session, such as saying prayers or reading the Scripture.
- Note that the session guides sometimes call for breaking into smaller groups or pairs. This gives everyone a chance to speak and participate fully. Mix up the groups; don't let the same people pair up for every activity.
- As always in discussions that may involve personal sharing, confidentiality is essential. Group members should never pass along stories that have been shared in the group. Remind the group members at each session: confidentiality is crucial to the success of this study.

Tips for Online Meetings

Meeting online is a great option for a number of situations. When circumstances preclude meeting in person, online meetings are a welcome opportunity for people to converse while seeing each other's faces. Online meetings can also expand the "neighborhood" of possible group members, because people can log in from just about anywhere in the world. This also give those who do not have access to transportation or who prefer not to travel at certain times of day the chance to participate.

One popular option is Zoom. This platform is used quite a bit by businesses. If your church has an account, this can be a good medium. Google Meet, Webex, and Microsoft Teams are other good choices. Individuals can obtain free accounts for each of these platforms, but there may be restrictions (for instance, Zoom's free version limits meetings to 40 minutes). Check each platform's website to be sure you are aware of any such restrictions before you sign up.

Video Sharing

For a video-based study, it's important to be able to screen-share your videos so that all participants can view them in your study session. The good news is, whether you have the videos on DVD or streaming files, it is possible to play them in your session.

- All the videoconferencing platforms mentioned above support screen-sharing videos. Some have specific requirements for assuring that sound will play clearly in addition to the videos. Follow your videoconferencing platform instructions carefully and test the video sharing in advance to be sure it works.

- If you wish to screen-share a DVD video, you may need to use a different media player. Some media players will not allow you to share your screen when you play copyright-protected DVDs. VLC is a free media player that is safe and easy to use. To try this software, download at videolan.org/VLC.
- *What about copyright?* DVDs like those you use for group study are meant to be used in a group setting in "real time." That is, whether you meet in person, online, or in a hybrid setting, Abingdon Press encourages use of your DVD or streaming video.
- *What is allowed:* Streaming an Abingdon DVD over Zoom, Teams, or similar platform during a small group session.
- *What is not allowed:* Posting video of a published DVD study to social media or YouTube for later viewing.
- If you have any questions about permissions and copyright, email permissions@abingdonpress.com.
- The streaming subscription platform Amplify Media makes it easy to share streaming videos for groups. When your church has an Amplify subscription, your group members can sign on and have access to the video sessions.
- Visit AmplifyMedia.com to learn more.

Training and Practice

- Choose a platform and practice using it so you are comfortable with it. Engage in a couple of practice runs with another person.
- Set up a training meeting.
- In advance, teach participants how to log in. Tell them that you will send them an invitation via email and that it will include a link for them to click at the time of the meeting.
- For those who do not have internet service, let them know they may telephone into the meeting. Provide them the number and let them know that there is usually a unique phone number for each meeting.
- During the training meeting, show them the basic tools available for them to use. They can learn other tools as they feel more confident.

During the Meetings

- **Early invitations.** Send out invitations at least a week in advance. Many meeting platforms enable you to do this through their software.
- **Early log in.** Participants should log in at least ten minutes in advance, to test their audio and their video connections.
- **Talking/not talking.** Instruct participants to keep their microphones muted during the meeting so extraneous noise from their location does not interrupt the meeting. This includes chewing or

yawning sounds, which can be embarrassing! When it is time for discussion, participants can unmute themselves. However, ask them to raise their hand or wave when they are ready to share, so you can call on them. Give folks a few minutes to speak up. They may not be used to conversing in web conferences.

SESSION 1

Overcoming Obstacles

Getting Ourselves Aligned with God

Planning the Session

Session Goals

- Identify four common barriers to hearing and understanding God's voice in our lives.
- Explore strategies for overcoming these barriers and opening ourselves to God's voice.
- Affirm that who we are is more important than what we do.

Biblical Foundation

- 1 Samuel 3:1-21

Preparation

- Read Chapter 1 of *On Purpose*, "Overcoming Obstacles: Getting Ourselves Aligned with God," by Jevon Caldwell-Gross.

- Read through this leader guide session in its entirety to familiarize yourself with the material being covered.

- Read the Biblical Foundation passage, 1 Samuel 3:1-21, especially verses 1-10 which are printed at the beginning of the book chapter.

- Contact group participants in advance and ask them to bring a journal or notebook as well as a pencil or pen. Your sessions each week will include time to reflect and write about your life and spiritual journey as a way of seeing how God might be speaking to you and leading you.

- Provide name tags, pens, extra notebooks, and Bibles for your group.

- Set up your DVD player or Amplify Media to watch the video segment.

Opening Activity and Prayer

Greet participants as they arrive, introducing yourself and welcoming them to the study. Invite them to fill out a name tag and pick up a Bible and a notebook if they did not bring their own.

When everyone has arrived, invite the group to introduce themselves, with each person stating their name, what they hope to learn in this study, and the most interesting place they have traveled.

When everyone has responded, discuss the following questions:

- Have you ever gotten lost? What happened? What did it feel like?
- How did you find your way back?
- How are you with directions? Do you feel confident getting from one place to another, or do you find it difficult?

Say: In this study, we are going to explore the book *On Purpose: Finding God's Voice in Your Passion*, where we'll open ourselves to God's voice and find purpose and meaning as we follow God's lead. The writer of this chapter, Jevon Caldwell-Gross, describes himself as "directionally challenged." That's why GPS navigation, which gives audible, turn-by-turn directions, is a gift that has made his life much easier. Wouldn't it be great if we had a spiritual GPS, with God telling us clearly how to get from point A to point B in our spiritual journey? Unfortunately, life doesn't work like that, but we can open ourselves to God's voice by eliminating barriers, practicing spiritual disciplines, surrendering our gifts and interests to God, and coming together with others. Today we'll explore barriers to hearing God's voice and how to overcome them.

Opening Prayer

Lead the group in the following prayer or one of your own:

Loving God, at times it can be hard to hear your voice. We want to live with purpose and meaning. We want to follow you, but so often it is hard to find the way. Yet even in these times we trust that you do speak. Open our ears and our hearts. Remove the barriers that prevent us from hearing your voice and fill us with your Holy Spirit so that we might follow your will and direction for our lives. In Jesus's name we pray. Amen.

Watch the Video

Play the Session 1 video for *On Purpose*, using the DVD or the Amplify Media streaming service.

Discuss:

- Did anything specific stand out as you watched the video?
- What is something you learned that you didn't know before?

Invite the group to keep both the video and the book in mind throughout the discussion below.

Study and Discussion

The Call of Samuel

Invite a volunteer to read 1 Samuel 3:1-10 (this is printed in *On Purpose*, pages 3–4). Discuss the following questions:

- How many times did the Lord call to Samuel? Why didn't Samuel recognize God's voice at first?
- What did Eli do to help Samuel understand what was happening? How did Eli's advice guide Samuel in responding to God?
- Have you ever sensed that God might be speaking to you? How did you know?
- What voices are speaking to you today? Think about all the voices you hear on a daily, weekly, and monthly basis.

Invite the group to take a few moments and list in their journals or notebooks the various voices they hear. These can be family members or friends, colleagues, authors, TV or internet personalities, or even advertisements. Allow time to write, then invite two or three members to share their responses. Discuss:

- Which of these might be voices through whom God can speak?
- How would you recognize if God were speaking to you through one of these voices?

Say: We hear a lot of voices today, some of which are helpful and good, and some of which are not. It can be challenging to recognize God's voice among these others, as the story of Samuel shows. But the story of Samuel also helps us see the things that stand in our way, and how we might overcome these obstacles to hear God's voice clearly.

Lack of Recognition

Read this quotation from *On Purpose*, chapter 1:

> Samuel's initial barrier was his inability to recognize God's voice. He heard God but was unsure of who was speaking....
>
> The lack of recognition is a familiar barrier. It's a test of our ability not just to hear what's been communicated but to determine whether this is God's prompting or something (or someone) else. We ask ourselves, "How do I know if this is God's voice?" (pages 10–11)

Jevon Caldwell-Gross also says that "recognition assumes a certain level of familiarity" (page 11), which requires both learning and patience.

- When have you had to learn a new skill? How did you go about doing it? How long did it take to master (maybe you are still working on it)?
- What was the role of practice as you learned this skill? What was the role of failure? Of learning from other people?
- What opportunities have you had to "practice" listening to God? What experiences have given you an opportunity to learn what God's voice sounds like?

Invite the group to write down their responses to this last question in their notebooks or journals. Allow them to write for a few minutes, then invite two or three group members to share. Discuss:

- What are some ways right now that you can practice listening and learn what God's voice sounds like in your life?

Say: Remember, Samuel failed more than once to recognize God's voice. In our spiritual lives, we too will fail, often more than once. Don't be discouraged but be patient with the process. Learning to identify God's voice takes time, just like learning anything else.

Dead Spots

Read the following quotation from *On Purpose*, chapter 1:

> Does it ever feel like you are in a spiritual dead spot—a place where it's hard to hear from God? Our faith journeys will undoubtedly include seasons or situations when hearing from God becomes difficult.... We check the lines of communication and realize that maybe the problem is not with the sender. Maybe we are not in a good place to hear from God. (pages 15–16)

Jevon Caldwell-Gross identifies two spiritual dead spots: distractions and disobedience. Discuss:

- What things in your life would you describe as distractions? Whether these are to-do lists or notifications or worries, what occupies your attention and prevents you from hearing God's voice?

- God spoke to Samuel at night, when he was lying down, with all distractions silenced. Where is your quiet place? When or where are potential distractions diminished, leaving space in your mind and heart for you to recognize God's voice?
- How can you intentionally devote more attention to God?
- Disobedience is another dead spot—times when we purposefully turn away from God and follow our own way. Have you ever found it difficult to hear God's voice because you were disobeying God?

Invite participants to answer this last question in their journals, writing about a time or times when they disobeyed God and found that God seemed distant or silent. Allow them to write for a few minutes, then invite two or three people to read their answers aloud.

Read the following quotation from *On Purpose*, chapter 1, then discuss the questions below:

> We often think of faith as our willingness to trust God. Obedience reveals how much God can trust us. Obedience is a discipline of showing God that we not only hear with our ears but also with our actions. (page 19)

- The more we listen and obey, the easier it becomes to hear God's voice. What can you do to obey God more faithfully?

- Where in your life right now do you feel tension between God's way and your own way? What would it mean for you to follow God's way?

Difficulty of Hearing Hard Things

Sometimes we pursue our own way because God says something we don't want to hear. In these cases, we act as if we don't hear God because God's voice is telling us a hard truth or calling us to a hard course of action.

Invite a volunteer to read aloud 1 Samuel 3:11-21. Discuss:

- What message did God give to Samuel? How do you think Samuel felt when he heard this message?
- Why was Samuel afraid to relay God's message to Eli?

Jevon Caldwell-Gross warns us about the temptation to be "always already listening," that is, listening to God with pre-determined understanding of what God will say. We want something pleasant or affirming, so we listen for those things and ignore other messages God might be trying to communicate to us.

- How can you open yourself to God's voice, including the things you may not want to hear?
- What is something God might be calling you to say or do that might be difficult? Is there a calling or nudging in your life that seems challenging or risky?

Invite participants to write their answers to these final questions in their journals or notebooks. After giving a few minutes to write, invites two or three people to share their responses.

- What would it mean for you to seriously consider this as a calling from God? What would happen if you answered God with obedience and a willingness to follow?

Closing Activity and Prayer

Mistaken Identity

The final barrier Jevon Caldwell-Gross identifies is "mistaken identity." This refers to the way our identity gets bound up with our calling and our responsibilities, leading us to the mistaken belief that "what we do" is the same as "who we are."

Read this quotation from *On Purpose*, chapter 1:

> When God gets the attention of Samuel, God does not bombard Samuel with a list of responsibilities or have an in-depth conversation about Samuel's calling. Instead, three times, God simply calls Samuel's name....
>
> With every call of Samuel's name, God affirms that Samuel is a child of God. (pages 25–26)

- Why do you think we place more emphasis on the tasks we are given versus the people we are called to become?

- What things or responsibilities have you attached to your identity and purpose?

Invite participants to write in their journals the following words:

"I am a child of God."

Remind them that whatever they do, whatever roles or responsibilities they have, they are children of God. It is within that identity that we all find our purpose. It is from that identity that God calls us in specific ways, but our worth and purpose do not depend on what we do.

Conclude your session by discussing the following questions:

- Which barriers do you often find are the most difficult to overcome as your listen for God's voice?
- What are the unique ways that God speaks to you? Are there spaces that you revisit to help amplify God's voice?

Closing Prayer

Close your session with the following prayer, or offer one of your own:

Eternal God, thank you for speaking to us. Thank you for creating us as your children and for calling us by name. We trust that it is in you and you alone that we find purpose, and we open ourselves to your word. By your Holy Spirit, remove every barrier that would prevent us from hearing your voice. Speak, Lord, for your servants are listening. Amen.

Raising Awareness

Practical Steps for Hearing God's Voice

Planning the Session

Session Goals

- Explore practical ways to listen for God's voice and discern God's will for our lives.
- Recognize the value of moving forward one step at a time, trusting God to lead us.
- Learn to pay attention to God's voice through: Scripture, Others, and Silence, as well as our subconsciouses.

Biblical Foundation

- Proverbs 2:1-11; 3:1-6

Preparation

- Read chapter 2 of *On Purpose*, "Raising Awareness: Practical Steps for Hearing God's Voice," by Magrey R. deVega.
- Read through this leader guide session in its entirety to familiarize yourself with the material being covered.
- Read the Biblical Foundation passages, Proverbs 2:1-11 and 3:1-6, which are printed at the beginning of the book chapter.
- Remind group participants to bring their journals or notebooks as well as a pencil or pen.
- Provide name tags, pens, extra notebooks, and Bibles for your group.
- Set up your DVD player or Amplify Media to watch the video segment.

Opening Activity and Prayer

Greet participants as they arrive, introducing yourself and welcoming them back to the study. Invite them to fill out a name tag and pick up a Bible and a notebook if they did not bring their own.

When everyone has arrived, invite any newcomers to introduce themselves and welcome them to the study. Open your discussion today with the following question:

- If you had a time machine, would you choose to go back to the past, or skip ahead to the future? Why?

Say: In today's session, we're going to explore the second chapter of *On Purpose: Finding God's Voice in Your Passion.* The writer of this chapter, Magrey R. deVega, begins by acknowledging that we cannot know the future. As much as we would like to know what will happen tomorrow, or several years from now, the future remains unknown. When we listen for God's voice, an important part of our listening must be a willingness to take things one step at a time, trusting God to reveal the way in God's own time. That's what it means to follow the words of Proverbs 3:5: "Trust in the LORD with all your heart; don't rely on your own intelligence."

Opening Prayer

Lead the group in the following prayer or one of your own:

God, we come to you for wisdom, insight, and understanding. We open our minds and lives to you, trusting you with all our hearts. Speak to us and guide us in listening for your voice through scripture, through others, and through silence. May your Holy Spirit be with us during our time together and help us to open ourselves more fully to your word and your voice. In Jesus's name we pray. Amen.

Watch the Video

Play the Session 2 video *for On Purpose*, using the DVD or the Amplify Media streaming service.

Discuss:

- Did anything specific stand out as you watched the video?
- What is something you learned that you didn't know before?

Invite the group to keep both the video and the book in mind throughout the discussion below.

Study and Discussion

Stepping Backward into the Future

Invite a volunteer to read the following quotation aloud from pages 35–36 of *On Purpose*:

> In William MacAskill's book *What We Owe the Future*, he says that every culture on earth thinks about the future as being in front of us, and the past as being behind us. Every culture, that is, except one. The Aymara, an indigenous people in Bolivia and Peru, think about the future as behind them, and the past as being in front of them. When they think about an event in the past, they point *ahead*. When they think about a possibility in the future, they point their thumbs *behind their back*.
>
> How does that make sense to them? Because they recognize that the past is the only thing they can see with clarity. That is not the case with the future. We don't have eyes on the back

of our heads, and we can't see the future clearly. The Aymara would say that in a way, all of us are walking backwards into the future.[1]

This is all to say that when it comes to being stuck in the past or trying to predict the future, the best way to live—perhaps the only way to live—is to focus on the present moment, which is the only thing we can know for sure.

Magrey R. deVega suggests that the first principle to open ourselves to God's voice is to focus on the present. Invite the group to spend a few moments answering the following two questions in their journals or notebooks:

- Where are you experiencing uncertainty about the future right now?
- What do you wish you could know in advance?

Allow time to write, then invite two or three members to share their responses and discuss them together. Then allow time for the group to answer the following question in their journals or notebooks:

- Magrey R. deVega writes, "When it comes to hearing God's voice and discovering God's purposes for us, we should only worry about the next faithful step that God has given us to take" (page 38). What is the next faithful step God is calling you to take as you consider this uncertain future?

---

1   William McCaskill, *What We Owe the Future* (Basic Books, 2022), 223-224.

After a few minutes, invite group members to share their responses.

Scripture

Magrey R. deVega recommends a simple acronym for helping us remember three ways God often chooses to speak to us: S.O.S., Scripture, Others, and Silence. By spending time regularly reading Scripture, listening to others we trust, and by spending time in silence, we can open ourselves to God's voice.

Discuss the following questions together:

- How often do you read Scripture?
- Do you have favorite biblical passages that you turn to frequently? What are they?
- How does God speak to you through passages you are familiar with?
- How might God speak to you through passages you are not familiar with?

Invite the group to consult "Bible Verses to Read in Times of Trouble," on pages 127–132 of *On Purpose*. These pages list a number of experiences and emotions that might prompt us to consult God's word.

- Which of these have you experienced most deeply in the past? Which of these, if any, are you experiencing right now?

Invite each person to look up and read silently one of the Scripture passages in a category they named. When everyone is finished, ask:

- How does your chosen passage encourage or teach you?

Conclude this section by reminding the group that reading the Bible each day, developing a daily habit of encountering God's word, is an important gift by which we can open ourselves to God's voice. God often speaks through Scripture. The more often we read it, the more we listen for God's leading.

Others

Read the following quotation from *On Purpose*, chapter 2:

> When we are seeking to hear God's voice in times of distress, we can best hear it in the company and companionship of other people (page 46).

Discuss:

- Who are the trusted friends, family members, or mentors you often turn to for advice or guidance?
- How often do you seek the wisdom of these or other people when you are wrestling with a difficult decision or facing something uncertain?
- When in the past has another person been a source of divine guidance for you?

- Who turns to you for advice? Have you ever
  considered that God might speak to others
  through you?

Say: The notion that God often speaks to us through others is a source of comfort and responsibility. We can turn to others to help us discern God's will, and we ourselves have the opportunity to help those around us better hear God's voice.

Magrey R. deVega describes the idea of a Clearness Committee on page 46. Invite the group to turn to that page and have a volunteer read the description of the Clearness Committee out loud. Note that the committee does not give advice but simply listens to the person seeking direction and asks questions to help them arrive at clarity.

If you have time, invite the group to try out the practice of a Clearness Committee in teams of two. Have each person find a partner (with one group of three if you have an odd number). One person will go first and explain to the other what kind of direction or guidance they are seeking from God. The other person will listen and ask questions, which the first person will answer aloud. Do this for three to five minutes, then switch.

When every pair is finished, bring the group back together and discuss:

- How was the experience for you? Was it helpful?
  Awkward? Uncomfortable?

- Did anyone receive a new insight or feel God's direction in any specific way?
- Is a Clearness Committee something you would like to try again with more people?

Silence

Magrey R. deVega describes several examples of people in the Bible who heard God's voice through silence. These include Elijah, Zechariah, and Jesus.

- Do you enjoy silence, or do you find it unnerving or distracting? Why?
- In addition to these biblical examples, Magrey R. deVega mentions a number of people who found inspiration or clarity through silence. Why do you think that is the case? What is the value of silence?

Magrey R. deVega implies that silence—pressing pause on our conscious mind—leaves room for our subconscious to work. This includes our dreams.

- Have you ever had a dream that led to an insight? What was the experience like? What did you discover in your dream? Why do you think you did not have this insight while you were awake?

Throughout the Bible, God speaks to people through dreams. These include Abraham, Jacob, Joseph, Daniel, Samuel, and many others.

- Do you believe God still speaks through dreams today? Why or why not?
- Have you ever felt like God spoke to you through a dream?
- Skim the sections "Why We Dream" and "Gaining Insight and Creativity" in *On Purpose*, pages 51–58. What do these sections teach you about how God might speak through dreaming and other aspects of our subconscious?
- How would you know if an insight from a dream came from God? What steps would you take to investigate it further and discern whether this really was God's voice?

Closing Activity and Prayer

Practical Steps for Hearing God's Voice

Read this quotation from *On Purpose*, chapter 2:

> This chapter has offered a handful of practical approaches you can follow to hear God's voice and discover God's purposes in your life. Take things one step at a time and pay attention to the in-between moments. Practice S.O.S., reading the Scriptures, listening with Others, and practicing Silence. And pay attention to the ways that God might be speaking through your subconscious, always checking those messages against the other ways God is speaking to you. (pages 57–58)

While God can and does speak in many ways, not just these, throughout the Bible and Christian history, God has often spoken to God's people through them.

- Which of these practical steps resonates most with you?
- Which of them do you find hardest to practice?
- How can you open yourself more fully to one or more of these steps in the week ahead?

Invite participants to choose one of these steps and write it down in their journal. Allow two to three minutes for everyone to write down what they can do in the week ahead to practice this step more intentionally. What do they hope to hear from God?

After everyone has written, allow two to three volunteers to share their response with the group. Affirm them and commit to pray for them as they seek God's voice in the week ahead.

Conclude your session by discussing the following questions:

- When has it been difficult for you to listen for God's voice one step at a time? Even when it was hard to do so, what were the benefits?
- How will you begin to apply the principles of Scriptures, Others, and Silence in your spiritual practices?

Closing Prayer

Close your session with the following prayer, or offer one of your own:

God, silence all voices but your own. Today and in the week ahead, we open our hearts and our minds to you. Speak to us through the pages of your word, through others, or through whatever way you choose to make your will known. We are ready to receive your direction and follow your voice. In Jesus's name. Amen.

SESSION 3

Channeling Our Passions

Discovering Our Gifts and Making a Difference

Planning the Session

Session Goals

- Recognize that we are affirmed, loved, and claimed by God, and this forms the foundation of our purpose and call.
- Name the difference between big-C Calling and little-c calling, and see that God can call us through many different means.
- Recognize how the affirmation of others can help us see our talents and gifts, and how we might call out the talents and gifts of those around us.

Biblical Foundation

- Luke 3:21-22
- Luke 4:16-21
- Matthew 2:1-12
- Matthew 4:18-22

Preparation

- Read chapter 3 of *On Purpose*, "Channeling Our Passions: Discovering Our Gifts and Making a Difference," by Sam McGlothlin.
- Read through this leader guide session in its entirety to familiarize yourself with the material being covered.
- Read the Biblical Foundation passage, Luke 3:21-22 which is printed at the beginning of the book chapter, and the others listed above.
- Remind group participants to bring their journals or notebooks as well as a pencil or pen.
- Provide name tags, pens, extra notebooks, and Bibles for your group.
- Set up your DVD player or Amplify Media to watch the video segment.

Opening Activity and Prayer

Greet participants as they arrive, introducing yourself and welcoming them to the study. Invite them to fill out a name tag and pick up a Bible and a notebook if they did not bring their own.

When everyone has arrived, ask:

- What is something that you do well? What are you good at? Don't be shy—own it!
- How do you know you're good at this thing? How long have you known?
- What do you do to practice or otherwise nurture and develop this talent?

Say: In today's session we're going to explore chapter 3 of *On Purpose*, "Channeling Our Passions: Discovering Our Gifts and Making a Difference." The writer of this chapter, Sam McGlothlin, helps us pay attention to our unique gifts, interests, and passions, and how God might be calling us to use them for God's kingdom. We'll learn to listen for the nudges and promptings of the Holy Spirit, and we'll explore what it would mean for us to surrender our gifts and talents to Jesus.

Opening Prayer

Lead the group in the following prayer or one of your own:

God, whatever gifts we have, whatever talents we possess come from you. You have made each of us good at something. Throughout our lives we have become familiar with things, we have developed interests and acquired skills, we have had experiences that have shaped us into who we are today. We trust, God, that you can speak to us through these things. Use our knowledge and skills to make yourself known to us and show us how we can use these things for your kingdom. It is in you that true purpose and meaning are found. Lord Jesus, we surrender ourselves to you. We are yours. Amen.

Watch the Video

Play the Session 3 video for *On Purpose*, using the DVD or the Amplify Media streaming service.

Discuss:

- Did anything specific stand out as you watched the video?
- What is something you learned that you didn't know before?

Invite the group to keep both the video and the book in mind throughout the discussion below.

Study and Discussion

Divine Deliveries

Read aloud the following quotation from chapter 3 of *On Purpose* (page 73):

> Callings happen to us and around us every day. These nudges can add up to our capital-C Calling. Or they can stand alone as our way to daily deliver the goodness of God's kingdom. There is no right or wrong, and they are not mutually exclusive. Both capital-C Callings and everyday callings (daily deliveries) lead to saving people, to

bringing more hope, healing, and wholeness to the world.

Discuss the following questions:

- Have you ever felt a nudge from the Holy Spirit that you believed you had to follow? What was the situation?
- Did you do what the Spirit was prompting you to do? What was the outcome?
- Have you felt a prompting from the Holy Spirit and chosen not to respond? Why not? What was the result of that situation?
- Are you feeling the Spirit prompting you in any way right now (not necessarily this moment, but throughout this study)?

Invite the group to write their answers to this last question in their journals or notebooks. Allow a few minutes to think and write, then invite two or three volunteers to share their responses aloud.

- Take a moment and write down the things you feel God may be calling you to do.

Big-C and Little-c Callings

Ask a volunteer to summarize the difference Sam McGlothlin describes between "Big-C" and "little-c" callings. Affirm that both are from God, and both are valuable for us and for the world. Discuss:

- Is your experience of the Spirit's leading and prompting more like a capital-C calling—a single, clear direction—or a series of opportunities to bring God's goodness to others?

Invite participants to draw a large letter C on a page of their journal or notebook. Ask them to think back through their lives and recall times when the Holy Spirit has prompted them to do something. Everyone should identify as many different instances as they can, and write them in short words and phrases around the large letter C.

Allow a few minutes for the group to reflect and write, then have them look for connections or patterns that emerge from these things. They can draw lines connecting events that are similar or seem otherwise related.

Allow the group several minutes to work on this in their journals, then invite two or three volunteers to share what they found. Encourage participants to spend more time doing this on their own after your study session. Discuss:

- How does this bring clarity or insight into what God might be calling you to do now or next?

Surrendering Our Gifts to Jesus

God often speaks to us through the things we know and love. Invite a volunteer to read Matthew 2:1-12. Read the following quotation from *On Purpose* aloud (pages 73–74):

> At the beginning of a New Year, many churches follow the journey of three magi who made their

way to worship Jesus. We don't really know if there were three of them, but we presume so because there were three gifts: frankincense, gold, and myrrh. What we do know is they were Gentiles. They were not waiting on a savior or messiah. They were people who studied the sky, likely Persian men from a priestly class known for dream interpretation and their knowledge of the stars.

…As these men, the magi, were doing what they knew, loved, and were trained to do, they saw something that glimmered in their eyes.

Discuss:

- What are the things you know and love?
- How might God speak to you through these things?
- When has someone else told you that you're good at something or have a talent? How has that affirmation shaped your identity and the way you feel about yourself? Has it informed your life choices at all?
- Think about the people in your life right now. What talents or special qualities do you see in them? How can you help them see the things they do well? What can you do to support them in this?

When the magi arrive, we are told they bow down and worship Jesus, placing their gifts at that tiny child's feet. This posture of surrender, of worship, cannot be overstated as we search for God's voice in our passions.

Invite a volunteer to read Matthew 4:18-22. Notice that although Jesus calls Simon, Andrew, James, and John to follow him and they leave their nets behind, they do not cease being fishermen. Instead, Jesus says to Simon and Andrew, "Come, follow me, and I'll show you how to fish for people."

Read the following quotation from *On Purpose* aloud (page 78):

> The good news after we give it all up is that Jesus holds on to what we know and love and repurposes it for the Kingdom. We don't really lose everything, it is just redirected. Jesus's tutelage, his on-the-job training, takes us from fishers of fish to fishers of people. Our gifts, interests, and passions cast a wider net than they once did, and we learn the best and worst spots to get a catch. God speaks to us in what we know and love, and we surrender these gifts of ours to Jesus. It is in that intersection of calling and surrender that our passions lead to God-given meaning and purpose.

Discuss:

- How might you surrender your gifts to Jesus? What would it mean for you to surrender the things you know and love to God—not giving them up, but offering them to Jesus for him to direct and use?
- What would it mean for your gifts, interests, and passions to "cast a wider net" than they do now? What opportunities can you envision if you were to give your interests and talents over to God?

What Brings You to Life? What Breaks Your Heart?

Sam McGlothlin says that a number of questions can help us identify the ways our gifts and passions point us to God's calling. Two of these questions are, "What brings you to life?" and "What breaks your heart?"

Invite a volunteer to summarize Sam McGlothlin's story about her first time preaching, under "What Brings You to Life?" on pages 81–84. Discuss:

- What brings you to life? When do you feel most alive and full of purpose and joy?
- What does it feel like when you are doing it?
- Is the answer to this question clear, or does it seem hard to identify one specific thing?

Invite the group to spend a few minutes writing in their journals or notebooks about what brings them to life. If they have a clear answer or several answers, have them write what these are and what they feel like. Why do they experience such joy and fulfillment through these things?

If they have no clear answer, invite them to imagine something new to try. Might God be leading them to explore something different and new? What would that be?

Allow a few minutes for the group to write, then invite two or three volunteers to share their responses with the group. Ask:

- What would it mean for you to surrender to God the thing that brings you to life?

Part of the scroll Jesus reads includes the words, "He has sent me to bind up the brokenhearted." Ask:

- What breaks your heart?
- Where do you see a need for healing and care? How might your interests and passions intersect with the hurt that you see and feel led to respond to?

Closing Activity and Prayer

Claimed, Commissioned, and Called by God

Ask a volunteer to read aloud Luke 3:21-22 and Luke 4:16-21. In his baptism, Jesus was claimed, commissioned, and called by God.

Read aloud the following quotation from *On Purpose* (page 69):

> I believe the same is true for us. If Jesus is claimed, commissioned, and called to preach good news, proclaim freedom, recover sight, liberate the oppressed, and proclaim the year of forgiveness, then as his followers we are sent to do the same. We are baptized as Jesus was. We receive the same Spirit that sent Jesus. It is by the same power of the Spirit that we are able to reject the evil powers of this world and renounce the spiritual forces of wickedness, seeking freedom and justice for all people.
>
> If that is the case, then *how* we do it is where our unique gifts, interests, and passions come in.

Discuss:

- Where do your gifts, interests, and passions intersect with the needs of the world?
- Where might God use your gifts and talents to
  bring good news, proclaim freedom, liberation,
  recovery of sight, and extend God's favor to those
  who need it most?
- What insights have you gained tonight about how
  God calls you through your own gifts, interests,
  and passions?

Closing Prayer

Close your session with the following prayer, or offer one
of your own:

*Loving God, thank you for claiming us, affirming us, and calling
us. Thank you for speaking to us through what we know and
love, through what brings us to life and what breaks our hearts,
through what others see in us. Lord Jesus, we thank you for our
gifts and interests, and we surrender them to you. We trust that
in your hands they will find their greatest purpose. In your holy
name we pray. Amen.*

Journeying Together

Joining with Others for Lasting Impact

Planning the Session

Session Goals

- Recognize that we may have many callings throughout our lives, and each of them is valid and a way to serve God.
- Affirm the role of others in helping us discern God's voice and recognize how we may help those around us see and understand God's will for their lives.
- Explore the ways other people contribute to us fulfilling God's call, and how supporting one another can lead to greater, lasting impact for God's kingdom.

Biblical Foundation

- Esther 4:8-16

Preparation

- Read chapter 4 of *On Purpose*, "Journeying Together: Joining with Others for Lasting Impact," by Susan Robb.
- Read through this leader guide session in its entirety to familiarize yourself with the material being covered.
- Read the Biblical Foundation passage, Esther 4:8-16, which is printed at the beginning of the book chapter.
- Remind group participants to bring their journals or notebooks as well as a pencil or pen.
- Provide name tags, pens, extra notebooks, and Bibles for your group.
- Set up your DVD player or Amplify Media to watch the video segment.

Opening Activity and Prayer

Greet participants as they arrive and welcome them to the study. Invite them to fill out a name tag and pick up a Bible and a notebook if they did not bring their own.

When everyone has arrived, ask and discuss the following questions:

- What is the most courageous thing you have ever done? What made it so?

- Would you ever do something like that again?
  Why or why not?

Say: In this fourth and final session, we will explore chapter 4, "Journeying Together: Joining with Others for Lasting Impact." The author of this chapter, Susan Robb, discusses how we often receive many calls from God throughout our lives, and that the input of others is a valuable gift to help us hear God's voice clearly, understand what it means, and discover what we should do in response. Through the story of Esther, we will learn that we both hear and respond to God's voice in community, and when we do so the impact is far greater than what we can achieve on our own. As we wrap up the study, we will name the things we learned, what we hope to gain greater clarity about, and how we can support one another on the journey going forward.

Opening Prayer

Lead the group in the following prayer or one of your own:

Dear God, you call us in many ways and many times throughout our lives. Few of us will receive only one call. Help us today to open our hearts and minds to what you are calling us to do next. If it is something new, give us understanding to see it clearly and courage to follow through. If we are already serving where you want us to be, give us affirmation and conviction, and show us how we might serve you with joy in a way that bears fruit. We long to hear your voice, Lord. Speak to us through others and use us to speak to those around us. In Jesus's name we pray. Amen.

Watch the Video

Play the Session 4 video for *On Purpose*, using the DVD or the Amplify Media streaming service.

Discuss:

- Did anything specific stand out as you watched the video?
- What is something you learned that you didn't know before?

Invite the group to keep both the video and the book in mind throughout the discussion below.

Study and Discussion

Many Callings

The author of this chapter, Susan Robb, describes her experience of feeling many different calls across her life. She has responded to each of these calls and sees God's hand in all of them. Invite a participant to read aloud the following quotation from *On Purpose* (page 93):

> In the past, I have been deeply intentional about discerning and pursuing the call to be a high school teacher, wife, mother, United Methodist minister, and author. Some of those calls were obvious and others were not (at least to me).

Discuss:

- Looking back over your life so far, would you say that you have a singular calling, or many?
- How have you discerned and pursued them (or it)?

Invite a volunteer to summarize Susan Robb's calling to attend seminary on pages 103-104 of *On Purpose.*

- How did the writer feel about this calling at first? What questions and hesitations did she have?
- What did she do to seek clarity?
- Have you received a calling that seemingly came "out of the blue" as something that felt crazy, impractical, or even dangerous? How did you respond?

When God's voice prompts us to something new, especially when it's unexpected, that experience can create feelings of both uncertainty and excitement.

- Is there something new you sense God is calling you to do or pursue?
- What thoughts and feelings do you have about it? What questions and hesitations do you have?
- What hopes and expectations do you have in regard to this new thing?
- How can you better discern this call?

Invite participants to spend a few minutes writing answers to this last set of questions in their journals or notebooks.

If they don't have a specific sense of God calling them to something new, they should ask what God may be calling them to do next in an area they are already serving. Allow a few minutes for everyone to write, then invite two or three volunteers to share their answers with the group.

Just Such a Time as This

Invite a volunteer to summarize the background information on Esther under the heading "A Time Such as This" (pages 97–102). Discuss:

- How did Esther's selection as queen change her circumstance? What opportunities and privileges might it have given her? What constraints did it place on her that she may not have had before?

Invite a volunteer to read Esther 4:8-16. Discuss:

- Mordecai wonders if Esther became queen "for a moment like this." What does he have in mind? What does he hope Esther will do?
- What does Esther risk if she agrees to do as Mordecai asks? What is at stake if she refuses?
- How does Esther go about fulfilling her calling? How does she involve the people around her? What roles do they play?
- Why do you think it was important for Esther to involve these others as she discerned what to do and put a plan into action?

Who Is Your Mordecai?

Invite a volunteer to read the following quotation from *On Purpose* aloud (pages 104–105):

> Sometimes, like Esther, we think we may have heard God's voice, but the call seems preposterous, or dangerous, or like the timing is just not right, so we need the clarity and encouragement—the voice—of someone else to recognize it. Just like Samuel needed Eli, and Esther needed Mordecai, I needed Ike's voice to confirm that this call was not crazy, or part of an imagination gone wild, but God's call.
>
> I've met many Mordecais (and Elis) in my life, and my guess is that you have as well. My high school English teacher offered clarity in my call to pursue a degree in education. A high school dance instructor encouraged me to utilize my passion in dance to work with high school girls. Friends and other ministers at the church helped me discern God's call to serve in various capacities and roles within the church, and to become an author.

Discuss:

- Who has been a "Mordecai" in your life? What mentors, friends, or others have helped you gain clarity when considering a big decision or some other aspect of God's call?
- Where might God be using others to speak to you now as you listen for God's voice?

Invite the group to spend a few minutes writing the names of their mentors and other influential people in their lives in their journals or notebooks. As they write each name, invite them to offer a simple, silent prayer of thanks for that person.

Allow a few minutes for people to write, then invite two or three volunteers to share the name of one important person and how that person served as a Mordecai for them.

Not only do we benefit from others to help us understand God's will. God also can use us to be a Mordecai for someone else.

- In your various roles, what gifts and what kinds of influence do you have in others' lives?
- How are you currently using your gifts and influence?
- How might God use you to bring clarity in someone else's call?

Fasting and Prayer

Before visiting the king, Esther asked the Jews in Susa to fast on her behalf, and she committed herself and her maids to fast as well.

- Why was fasting so important? What do you think the three-day fast accomplished?
- Fasting and praying often occur together in the Bible. What do you imagine Esther prayed for during this time?

- What are you praying for now as you seek to hear God's voice? What direction or insight are you hoping God will bring?

Coming Together with Others

Invite a volunteer to read aloud the story of Amy's Friends (now called New Friends New Life) on pages 113–114. Discuss:

- What did the group of women do to support the woman who was crying after church?
- What was God's call initially in this situation? Whom did God call? How did they hear and respond to it?
- How did God's call shift and change over time? Who else responded to God as the need and opportunity to serve expanded?
- How would you describe the difference it made for an entire community to work together instead of just one or two people working alone?

Read the following quotation from *On Purpose* aloud (pages 112–113):

> Esther and Mordecai's decree inspires all in the Jewish community to work together to thwart the evil plans of those who would seek their destruction.
>
> The wisdom Esther gleans from the fasting (and prayers) of the community helps her approach the king in a way that reinforces his love and favor.

One well-timed conversation leads to another and ultimately leads to Esther and Mordecai inspiring the community to work together for their salvation. Their praying together and working together changes the trajectory of all of their lives and changes the trajectory of a nation. Together, through God's grace, they accomplish what they never could have done alone.

Discuss:

- The people around Esther not only help her hear God's voice. She and they help one another to fulfill God's purpose.
- As you consider your own calling, who can come alongside you? What help do you need, or how can partnership with others open the door for greater impact?
- How can you work together with someone else to help them fulfill their call from God?
- What can your small group do to strengthen and support one another as you continue to hear and respond to God's voice?

Closing Activity and Prayer

What's Next?

This is the final session of the study. As you close, ask the group to think over the past four weeks and identify the things they have learned during your time together. Invite the group to look through their journals or notebooks and discuss the following questions:

- What barriers have you identified in your life that stand in the way of hearing God's voice clearly?
- What practices have you identified to open yourself more intentionally to God's voice?
- What have you learned about your gifts, interests, passions, and how God might seek to use them for God's purposes?
- What have you heard from God during this time?

Invite the group to spend a few minutes writing in their journals or notebooks their answers to the following questions:

- Has the Holy Spirit brought you any clarity, direction, or sense of conviction through this study?
- What do you sense God wants you to do next? Write down any next steps in your journal or notebook. Be as specific as possible. (You may see many next steps, or only one or two.)
- What would it mean for you to take this next step? What would you have to risk to do it? What opportunities would it open up for you? What doors would it close?
- What would it mean if you choose not to take this step?
- Who else would be involved if you take this step? What would they have to do or give up? What

would they gain? How do you need their support and encouragement?

Allow a few minutes for everyone to write, then invite two or three volunteers to share what stood out for them. Encourage the group to continue reflecting on these questions in the days ahead. Encourage each person to follow through and take action.

Closing Prayer

Close your session with the following prayer, or offer one of your own:

Eternal God, thank you for speaking to us. Thank you for calling us by name and for showing us what keeps us from hearing your voice clearly. Thank you for speaking to us through Scripture, others, and silence. Thank you for the unique gifts, interests, and passions you have placed in our lives. And thank you for the people around us, who can support us and whom we can support as we all seek to follow your call. Continue to speak, Lord. Give us wisdom, understanding, and courage. And above all help us to trust that we are loved, that we belong to you, and that who we are will always be more important than what we do. Lord Jesus, we love you. In your name we pray. Amen.

**Watch videos
based on
*On Purpose:
Finding God's Voice
in Your Passion*
through
Amplify Media.**

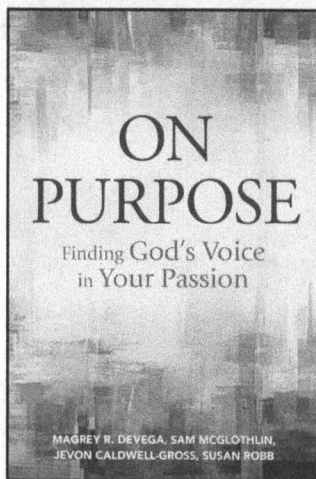

Amplify Media is a multimedia platform that delivers high quality, searchable content with an emphasis on Wesleyan perspectives for churchwide, group, or individual use on any device at any time. In a world of sometimes overwhelming choices, Amplify gives church leaders and congregants media capabilities that are contemporary, relevant, effective and, most importantly, affordable and sustainable.

With *Amplify Media* church leaders can:

- Provide a reliable source of Christian content through a Wesleyan lens for teaching, training, and inspiration in a customizable library
- Deliver their own preaching and worship content in a way the congregation knows and appreciates
- Build the church's capacity to innovate with engaging content and accessible technology
- Equip the congregation to better understand the Bible and its application
- Deepen discipleship beyond the church walls

Ⓐ AMPLIFY. MEDIΛ

**Ask your group leader or pastor about Amplify Media
and sign up today at www.AmplifyMedia.com.**

Watch videos
based on
OnPurpose:
Turning Your Vision
into Your Passion
through
Amplify Media

AMPLIFY MEDIA

CPSIA information can be obtained
at www.ICGtesting.com
Printed in the USA
LVHW031518140623
749701LV00005B/8

9 781791 029715